ADVANCED CREDIT REPAIR
SECRETS REVEALED

THE DEFINITIVE GUIDE TO REPAIR AND BUILD YOUR CREDIT FAST

BY

Marsha Graham

TABLE OF CONTENTS

Disclaimer

The Author has aimed to be accurate and complete in the publication of this book. However, the author assumes no responsibility for any errors or incompleteness in this material. This book offers no guarantee that you will get a particular result from using the material within, also individual results may vary based on individual circumstances. The author is not liable for any risk or loss from the use of the material in this book. Users of this publication should use their judgment regarding their particular use and application of this material within. This book is not written to be used as a source of legal, accounting, finance and business advice.

INTRODUCTION

THE IMPORTANCE OF GOOD CREDIT

Do you have bad credit? Is your credit score below 620? Is it hard to live the life you really want?

If this sounds like you, you're not alone. Over 40 million Americans share your pain and frustration. Without good credit, you'll find it nearly impossible to qualify for a mortgage or a car loan. Bad credit often robs people of their dreams: starting a business, attending school, or finding a good job.

Is there hope? What can this book do for you?

Yes – there is always hope! It can be hard to accept the fact that you need credit repair, but with the information in this book, you can establish good credit and live the lifestyle you desire. Millions of people just like you have paid thousands of dollars for the information I'm about to reveal to you. However, this book lets you in the *secrets of the credit repair pros* – for a fraction of the cost!

Why write a book about credit repair? Why is good credit so important?

Good question! Like you, I know what it's like to have less than perfect credit. However, I'm here to tell you that you can change your credit history and the direction of your life. The techniques you're about to learn are the closely guarded secrets that credit repair experts use to remove countless negative items from their clients' credit reports – often in 30 days or less!

Your credit score governs many aspects of your financial situation. It has a huge impact on your quality of life and determines if you qualify for many life-changing opportunities:

- A New Apartment in a Better Location – and the Utilities You Need!

- The Mortgage on Your Dream Home

- A New Car Loan - and even Lower Auto Insurance Rates!

- Refinance Your Existing High-Interest Loans

- Credit Cards with Lower Rates and More Perks

- Student Loans and Business Loans to get a Fresh start on Life and Your Career

Remember - developing and maintaining great credit is like having money in the bank!

What if you've made mistakes in the past?

Let's face it, we all want good credit; however, things can happen in life that are out of our control. The one constant of life is change: marriages can end in divorce, people can lose their jobs, and health issues can drain your savings. These life changes can result in bad credit for many people.

No matter what your situation, you deserve a fresh start!

It's time to learn from your mistakes, get back on your feet, and move on with your life. The solution is simple; we all want the best things in life for ourselves and our families. Don't wait - Read this book today and discover my secret methods for easily transforming bad credit into good – and getting the lifestyle you deserve!

THE UNBELIEVABLE BENEFITS OF GOOD CREDIT

What can you expect when you have excellent credit?

You can expect to receive credit card preapprovals with 0% introductory rates on purchases, balance transfers, and excellent reward programs. You'll also receive offers to increase your credit card limits.

Did you know people with great credit can fly for free?

Yes, it's true – travelers can exchange their credit card reward points for plane tickets, or even for cash!

When you restore your credit and start building a good reputation, you'll get attractive credit card offers for cash back, gift cards, monthly free credit scores, no annual fees and much more.

Would you like to make major purchases with little or no down-payments?

Good credit also puts you in a position to save money on your purchases. It costs significantly more to borrow when you have poor credit. When you repair your credit, you'll be able to qualify for lower interest rates, which can help you lease a car for less, obtain a better mortgage, or get a credit card with a lower APR.

With the advice in this book, you'll save money every time you finance a car, buy a house, or purchase anything else on credit.

Do you dream of quitting your "dreaded day job"?

With the amazing credit tips in this book, you can get the financing you need to start your own business and be your own boss!

Did you know good credit can even help you find a life partner?

Most people want to share their lives with someone who has a good financial reputation. Good credit increases your chances of owning a home, saving money, and starting a family. Credit can help you open a college fund account for your kids and travel the world with your partner. You can offer your "other half" the peace-of-mind of knowing you can care for them if they lose their job, become ill, or want to spend more time with your children.

You will be more attractive and confident when you repair your credit. Read this book, follow these simple tips, and improve your self-esteem - today!

What Are the "Dollars and Sense" of Good Credit?

If you're the kind of person who needs to "see the numbers", take a look at this example of how a high credit rating helps you save big:

If your credit card had a balance of $10,000, an interest rate of 21%, and a monthly payment of approximately $225, it would take you 87 months to pay it off in full. By this time, you would have paid $10,068 in principal and $9,507 in interest.

However, you can save time and money by reducing your interest rate. Imagine you've read this book, followed my instructions, and built up a good credit score and credit history. In a short time, you qualify for a credit card with a lower interest rate, and rollover your $10,000 balance onto this new card.

For the sake of example, let's that your new credit card has a 7% interest rate and you keep paying $225 per month as you did with your old card.

By the time you pay off your debt, you will have paid only $10,091 in principal and $1609 in interest. Also, you will be debt-free in only 52 months.

Wow! In this example, you saved $7,898 in interest payments and three years of your life!

What if you have mortgage debt? Will this method work for you?

Absolutely! Let's take a look at another example:

Suppose you have a $185,000 mortgage with a 30-year fixed 8% interest rate and a monthly payment of $1357.45. Now imagine having the same 30-year $185,000 mortgage with a 6% interest fixed rate.

Your monthly payment would be only $1109.17, saving you $89,000 over the remaining term of your mortgage!

How can you escape the trap of bad credit?

Let me take you by the hand and help you escape your debt - we can get you started right away! Bad credit costs you a lot of money – and the best years of your life! You deserve to get good credit right now without paying hundreds or even thousands of dollars to a credit repair expert.

What can you do to start saving big today?

In the first chapter of this book, I give you an in-depth look into the details of credit repair, how to establish and build you credit, and how protect the good credit you've established.

Read this book, follow my tried-and-tested advice, and save big as you get a fresh start on life!

CHAPTER 1

THE VALUE OF CREDIT

What is credit? Credit can be defined as the use of someone money to obtain goods or services before payment. Credit is also a financial obligation that has to be paid in the future; credit is also based on trust that the borrower will make payment to the lender in the future. There are three major credit agencies in the USA, which keeps a file that contains each consumer financial data. These companies are credit bureaus, and their names are Equifax, Experian, and Transunion. Credit Bureaus use a scoring model to help determine a borrower creditworthiness; this scoring system is a measure of your credit. Your ability to borrow money is often based on the information in your credit report otherwise known as your credit file.

What type of information is in your credit report? Your credit report usually contains identifying information such as your name, address, date of birth, and your place of employment. Your credit report lists the types of credit you use, account balances, the length of time your accounts has been open, and if you pay your bills on time. Your credit report also contains inquiries, collection items, judgments, charge off items, bankruptcies, foreclosure, late payments, repossessions, and liens.

YOUR CREDIT SCORE

Your credit score is a numerical figure based on information in your credit report. Most lenders use your credit score as a measurement of your credit worthiness.

The most common scoring model is the "Fico Score", the FICO score was developed by the Fair Isaac Corporation to help determine a person credit risk. The FICO score ranges from 300 to 850, and the FICO scoring system is used by the three major credit bureaus: Equifax, Experian, and Transunion.

WHAT FACTORS DETERMINE YOUR CREDIT SCORE?

Payment history is the number one component when calculating a person credit score. Payment history makes up approximately 35% of your credit score. Your ability to repay your debts promptly can have a tremendous impact on your credit score.

Debt Owed =30% of your credit score

The next important component in determining your credit score is the "Amount of debts owed as reflected on your credit report. The debt owed accounts for 30% of your credit score. The more debt you owe on your accounts, and the higher the percentage of your credit card utilization, the higher your credit risk. Also, the amount of debt owed on particular types of accounts, particularly credit cards (revolving credit accounts) can have a tremendous impact on your credit. Typically, 33% or more of a debt owed on your total available revolving credit limit will have an adverse effect on your credit score.

Length of credit history = 15% of your credit score

The length of your credit history determines 15% of your credit score. Credit history takes into account the length of time since you opened your credit account, the particular types of accounts you have, such as credit cards, student loans, and a mortgage.

The length of your credit history is used as a guide to predict how you will use credit in the future. Therefore, older credit accounts are taken into consideration by lenders than more recent credit accounts. Closing your older credit accounts can have a negative impact on your credit score because your older credit accounts are essentially a significant part of your credit history.

Account Mix = 10% of your credit score

The different types of accounts you have on your credit reports such as installment loans, credit cards, mortgage, and student loans will help determine your credit risk. By having a mix of credit accounts on your credit report, you can contribute to increasing your credit score. Lenders will also be able to better determine if you are adept at handling various types of debts.

New Credit Mix= 10% of your credit score

New credit accounts are determined by the number of recently opened accounts and the number of your recent credit requests. Be careful not to open too many credit accounts frequently, because this may put you in a high-risk category to potential lenders and cause your credit score to become lower.

CREDIT SCORE GUIDE

A 750 or higher credit score is excellent! If your credit score is well above the average score of U.S. consumers, then you will mostly qualify for the lowest rates on loans and credit cards.

A 720 to 750 credit score is very good. If your credit score is above the average score of U.S. consumers, then lenders will consider you to be a good risk, and you would most likely qualify for a lower interest rates on loans.

A 660 to 720 credit score is good. If your credit score is close to the national average score of U.S. consumers and most lenders, consider this a good score.

A 560 to 659 credit score is fair. However, your credit score would fall below the average score of U.S. consumers, some lenders will approve loans with this score, but mostly likely you will pay much higher interest rates for monies borrowed.

A credit score lower than 560 is considered bad. If your credit score is well below the average score of U.S. consumers, then lenders might determine that you are a high-risk borrower, and you may find it very hard to obtain credit.

CHAPTER 2

DISCOVER THE SECRETS TO ESTABLISH CREDIT IN 30 DAYS OR LESS

How can I get credit if I do not have a credit history? Establishing credit can be a daunting task, but we will reveal some simple ways to get credit fast!

Step#1 Apply for a secured credit card with a financial institution that offers one.

Getting approved for a secured card will be easier than getting approved for an unsecured card because you will be required to make a monetary deposit to get your credit card. Also, make sure the financial institution you applied for a secured credit with will report your information to the credit bureaus.

Step#2 The piggyback system: is defined as using someone else credit account to help establish your credit history. For example, a married couple named John and Jane has two entirely different credit histories. John has five unsecured credit cards for over ten years, two store cards for over five years and an auto loan for the past two years. Jane on the other does not have any credit account what so ever; in fact, Jane was been declined twice in six months by creditors when she applied for two unsecured credit cards.

John then calls one of his credit card companies and requested for his wife Jane to be a joint account, holder. The credit card company sent a form which required John and Jane signatures, personal information and a clear copy of their ID.

Two weeks later Jane received her first unsecured credit card in the mail and instantly established her credit profile. Soon after Jane credit report was updated to reflect her credit account that showed ten years of on time payments. Jane began receiving fantastic credit offers in the mail. The credit card offers Jane received are for zero percent interest rate plus tons of points and cash back!

Step#3 Make sure you always make all your payments on or before the due date.

Step#4 Make sure to keep your credit card balance at 33% or lower of your total credit limit.

Step#5 Wait at least six months before you apply for an unsecured card. Because you do not want too many inquiries on your credit report, this will reduce your credit score and signal to potential lenders that you are credit hungry.

Step#6 When applying for your first unsecured card you may want to know your chances of getting this card. You can visit http://www. creditcards.com/credit-card-news/application-odds-approval-1267.php to get an insight of your odds of being approved for a particular credit card you desire.

Also, most creditors report new credit accounts to the credit bureaus on a monthly basis. Therefore, if your new account is not being reported to the credit bureau by your creditor, then you should immediately contact your creditor and ask them to do so promptly.

Step#7 After obtaining your second credit card you may want a mix credit profile; therefore you should apply for an unsecured retail card within the next six months. Having mixed credit accounts will enhance your profile to potential lenders. Because potential lenders will see that you are capable of managing various types of credit.

Eventually, as the needs arise, you can apply for an installment loan because having an installment loans show a certain level of experience with handling credit. Installment loans such as car loans usually have a fixed monthly payment which requires more discipline to maintain your payments.

Another way to build your credit is owning a home; you can create a strong credit history by making on time mortgage payments. Having a mortgage suggests that you are more financially stable and capable of handling bigger loans.

OTHER BENEFITS OF OWNING A HOME

You can take advantage of the tax benefits of owning a home. Specifically, you can deduct mortgage interest and real estate property taxes on your tax return. Also as your mortgage decreases and your property value increases your equity will grow.

Owning a home is part of the American dream and to some people it might seem unattainable. However, did you know to qualify for a mortgage as a first-time home buyer you only need a credit score of 620 and a 3.5% money down payment? Also, most states offer mortgage programs for first-time home buyers, mortgage programs that provide flexible underwriting guidelines, no prepayment penalties, and down payment assistance.

To learn more about these offers just Google programs for first-time home buyers and the name of your (state). You will uncover a wealth of information that may be of tremendous financial benefit to you and your family.

CHAPTER 3

UNCOVER THE LITTLE KNOWN SECRETS TO REPAIR BAD CREDIT FAST!

Let's face it we all want to own a nice car, own a beautiful home or have access to capital to start or grow a business. Whatever our financial desires are sometimes we need to borrow money to reach them. Some people credit was ruined because of one or more of the following reasons:

- They lost their job
- They were the victim of identity theft
- Inaccuracies in their credit report
- They filed for bankruptcy
- They got a divorce
- They went through a foreclosure
- Repossession
- Judgments
- Loan Default
- Late Payments
- Medical bills
- Tax liens
- Student loans

They have miscellaneous items such as delinquent utility bills being reported on their credit report.

Now that we have identified some of the most common causes of bad credit how we restore our credit?

Step 1

DEBT VERIFICATION

The verification method is one of the most powerful closely guarded secrets used by most credit repair companies. What exactly is the verification method and how can you use this simple process to restore your credit?

Under the Fair Credit Reporting Act, you have the right to investigate the information in your credit report. You can obtain a free copy of your credit report once annually from the three major credit bureaus: Equifax, Transunion, and Experian or you can get a free copy of your credit from www.annualcreditreport.com.

It is important to obtain a copy of your report from all three credit bureaus because your credit report may vary from one credit bureau to another.

Once you receive a copy your credit report, you should review it very carefully for any inaccurate information such as late payments, charge off accounts, collection items and any other erroneous items.

If you have identified any incorrect item on your credit report, you should send a letter to the credit bureau requesting a verification of the debt. Under the FCRA, the credit bureau has 30 days to investigate and respond to your debt verification request. Also, if you send additional information within the 30 day period to the credit bureau, they will have 45 days to investigate and respond to you. The credit bureau would also have 45 days to investigate and respond to you if you used www.annualcreditreport.com to obtain a copy of your credit report.

You can file a lawsuit against the credit bureau in court for up to $1000 if they do not respond to you in that particular time frame.

Also, the federal Fair Credit Reporting Act (FCRA) promotes the accuracy, fairness, and privacy of information in the files for each consumer at the credit reporting agencies. Therefore, you have the right to know what is in your file.

You also have the right to ask for a credit score, you have the right to dispute incomplete or inaccurate information found in your credit report, consumer reporting agencies must correct or delete inaccurate, incomplete, or unverifiable information within 30 days, consumer reporting agencies may not report outdated negative information, and you may be able to sue a consumer reporting agency violates the Fair Credit Reporting Act in a state or federal court.

STEP 2

WHAT IF THE DEBT VERIFICATION DIDN'T WORK?

You should do a re-verification. You can send a letter to the credit bureau requesting them to provide you with the particular method they used to verify the debt. You should ask the credit bureau to provide you with the names of the person they contacted during the verification, you can ask for addresses and any other relevant information that describes the procedure used in their investigation. You can ask the credit bureau to comply with the FCRA laws by making sure that they are reporting accurate information on your credit report and expedite your request for a re-verification. Also, please make sure you have additional new information to present to the credit bureau regarding the case you are re-investigating. Because your re-investigation will be deemed as frivolous if you are disputing the same item without providing new evidence to support your claim.

WHAT IS E- OSCAR

The main reason to ask the credit bureau how was your verification conducted is because of e-OSCAR. E-OSCAR is a computerized system that allows the credit bureaus to respond to a consumer credit disputes automatically. The credit bureau will change your dispute into a numerical code, the numerical code summarizes the consumer's dispute. The credit bureau then sends the code to the creditor and asks them to verify it. The creditor would then state whether the code is accurate or not. Mainly the e-OSCAR method may minimize your detailed dispute that may include documented evidence into a two or three digit code. The problem with this approach is that it may not conduct an investigation in a thorough manner. Also, it is up to the credit bureau employee to choose a code that accurately describe your dispute and the documented evidence you sent to support your investigation might get condensed into a code.

HOW TO FORCE THE CREDIT BUREAU TO CONDUCT A PROPER DISPUTE?

You have the right to ask the credit bureau what method was used to investigate your dispute; you are given this right by the Fair Credit Reporting Act. If the credit bureau sends you information stating that your dispute has been verified, you can ask them how the dispute was conducted. Also you can write or call the original creditor for proof the negative information on your credit report belong to you and that information is being accurately reported. If the original creditor cannot provide evidence that this information belongs to you, then you can consider suing the credit bureau. But before you look to pursue legal action, it is wise to send the credit bureau the proof you contacted the original creditor along any correspondence you received from the original creditor that may support your dispute. Also, inform the creditor you have a right to sue them for reporting inaccurate information on your credit report, and you intend to proceed with legal action. Give the credit bureau at least 30 days to respond to you before you decide to take any further action.

ONLINE DISPUTE VS DISPUTE BY MAIL

Online credit bureau disputes usually offer limited options for you to express the reasons for your dispute entirely. For example, online disputes often come with preselected choices for you to pick from to categorize your dispute. The online dispute systems often limit the options of the user, the user then often makes a selection that may hinder the dispute process.

Mailing your dispute offer you the opportunity to fully express the reasons why you think items on your credit report are inaccurate and sending your dispute by mail enhance your ability to include proof to support your dispute.

It is also important to note that you should keep a copy of all correspondence between you and the credit bureau, and you should also send all of your letters to the credit bureau by registered mail.

Step 3

THE DISPUTE METHOD

If there is an obvious erroneous item on your credit report, you can outright send a letter to the credit bureau asking them to remove the inaccurate item. The same procedures and formality apply to this method as the verification method. You are stating that the erroneous item on your credit report does not belong to you.

HOW TO REMOVE COLLECTION ITEMS FROM YOUR CREDIT REPORT?

You have just finished a hard day of work; as soon as you get home you do what most Americans do….you check your mail. You notice a bright yellow envelope with bold writing stating URGENT BUSINESS MATTER, OPEN IMMEDIATELY! Upon opening the letter, you learn that a collection company is demanding you pay a debt you owe by a particular time. In addition to that the debt collection company is threatening to ruin your credit. You know this debt does not belong to you, but you feel helpless. What can you do? In a situation like this you are working against time because the debt collector can report you to a credit bureau after 30 days.

Don't Panic

As a consumer, you have the right to validate the debt under the Fair Debt Collection Practices Act. Therefore, if you received a letter from a collection agency requesting you pay a debt you are not aware of you should ask for a debt validation.

It is possible you may have originally owed a debt to a lender, but it does not mean the collection agency attempting to collect the debt from you owns the debt.

Next Step

Write a letter to the collection agency requesting a validation of the debt if the debt cannot be validated then the debt collector is not allowed to collect the debt or contact you. The Fair Credit Act does not permit the collection agency to place the debt on your credit report if they cannot validate it.

You Can Sue

If the debt collection agency violates any FCRA laws, you can also sue the collection agency for up to $1000 in damages for each time the debt collector violate your rights.

THE DAMAGE IS ALREADY DONE: A COLLECTION HAS BEEN REPORTED TO YOUR CREDIT REPORT.

You passed a car dealership one evening and saw the car of your dreams, so you decided to go in and inquire about the cost of the car.

The sales person told you the price of the car is $25,000, but you have the option of financing the vehicle. You thought to yourself that this is a great option for you because you cannot afford to pay for the car in full at this stage in your life. So after going home you did a lot of thinking, you decided to return to the car dealership and apply for a CAR LOAN. Dave, the friendly car sales rep, verified your identity then proceeded to run your credit and apply for the car loan, Dave hit submit to process your request. Dave computer screen states this will take a minute please wait….within seconds Dave said sorry but, unfortunately, the bank could not approve your application due to a poor credit history. You are shocked because you have always paid your bills on time, and you are not aware of any negative item on your credit report.

Later on that night you decided to get a free copy of your credit report at www.annualcreditreport.com. You were shocked to learn that a company by the name of John Doe ABC bill collector reported you owing them $15000. What the bananas? You thought this must be a mistake or fraud. How can you remove this collection item from your credit report?

SOLUTION

You should send a letter to each of the credit bureaus reporting the collection item. Here is an example what your letter might look like:

Your name

Date of Birth

current address

SS#

Report number

Date

Dear Madam/Sir

John Doe Collection item is being reported on my credit report. I am exercising my right under the Fair Credit Report Act to dispute this inaccurate item on my credit report.

Please investigate this item and remove it as soon as possible

Thank You

Yours Truly

What if the credit bureau refuses to remove the collection item?

The credit bureau by law will respond to your request within 30 days upon receiving your dispute letter. Finally after 20 days you received a letter from the credit bureau stating that the collection item has been verified. In other words, the credit bureau is indicating the collection item belongs to you. What further actions can you take to remove this collection Item?

Answer

Under the Fair Credit Reporting Act, you can sue the credit reporting agency for reporting inaccurate information on your credit report after you requested them to correct it.

Now, before you begin to file a lawsuit against the credit bureau. You may want to inform them that you are aware of your rights under the FCRA to sue them for reporting inaccurate information on your credit report. You can explain to the credit bureau the kind of the negative impact this collection item is having on your life. For example, you can tell them if you have denied credit and the financial restrictions this has caused you. You may want to ask the credit bureau to reinvestigate the matter and to provide you with a detailed account of how the investigation was conducted.

LEARN HOW TO AVOID A FRIVOLOUS CREDIT DISPUTE

A word of caution when it comes to disputing items on your credit report, the credit bureau reserves the right not to investigate frivolous disputes. A frivolous dispute is when a consumer asks the credit bureau to investigate an item numerous times without offering any new evidence to support the request. Also challenging every single item on your credit report all at once can be considered to be frivolous.

If your dispute comes back as verified, you should try fully to understand the reason the credit bureau came to that determination. Try to gather as much proof to support your dispute then wait 3 to 4 months then file another dispute.

HOW TO SETTLE YOUR DEBT WITH YOUR ORIGINAL CREDITOR?

Life can be filled with huge obligations and excessive financials burdens, so it is not surprising many people become over 90 days past due on their credit accounts.

Once faced with this dilemma some people opt to ignore their bills totally until the problem just disappear. However, this is may not be the best solution for a problem that can drag your credit score down into the gutter. If your credit card is beyond 150 days past due the creditor will most likely sell your debt to a collection company. Therefore, you have an opportunity to negotiate your debt with your creditor before a debt collection company purchases your debt. Before you call your lender, be prepared to have an honest conversation with your creditor and to give an explanation why you are seeking to settle your debt. Secondly, you should have a clear objective in mind as to what you are expecting to accomplish from your negotiation with your creditor. Here are some things you may want to consider prior to going into a negotiation with your lender. You can ask your creditor to remove the late payment comments from your credit report in exchange for a particular payment. You might want to ask your lender to list your account as paid in full and to exclude all negative comments from your credit report. You should make notes to track whom you spoke with from your creditor's company, time, date and the specifics of the agreement.

PAY FOR DELETE

What if you asked a credit bureau to verify if a debt belongs to you? The credit bureau then verified the item as belonging to you. After looking further into the matter, you suddenly realized that you did, in fact, owe the debt, but you recalled owing only $500 as oppose to $1500. What can you do? You can contact the debt collector and ask them to remove the item from your credit report by a particular time and for a certain amount of money. Also, you should send all your communication to the creditor via registered mail. You should specify in your letter to the debt collector that your agreement is final, and your agreement is a binding contract.

You should ask the debt collector to send you a signed letter agreeing to delete the item for a specific amount of money, and by a particular time. Please note debts are usually settled for 30% to 40% less than the original amount of the debt.

BENEFITS OF SETTLING YOUR DEBTS

- Restore your credit rating.

- Qualify for lower interest loans and credit cards.

- Avoid harassing calls from creditors and debt collectors.

- You can make affordable payments, and your privacy can be protected by possibly avoiding bankruptcy.

A word of caution, you may have to engage in several rounds of negotiation to reach a debt settlement agreement. Here is an example of the process. Step one send an initial letter to the debt collector with an offer to settle your debt for a specified amount of money along with any other favorable terms for you and the debt collector.

Here is an example of what your letter to the debt collector should like:

Sample debt settlement letter

Your name

Address

Phone number

Debt collection company name

Address

To whom it may concern

Account number

I would like an opportunity to resolve this outstanding debt owed to your company as soon as possible. I am offering x amount of dollars to settle my debt entirely.

Also, I would like you to remove all late payments comments associated with this debt from my credit report.

I may not be able to make another offer such as this one because of my current financial obligations.

If you agree to the terms of this letter, then please sign it and return a copy of it to me. Once I receive a signed copy of this letter then I will pay you x amount of dollars in the form of a bank check or money order.

Thank You

Yours Truly

HOW TO QUICKLY REMOVE AN OUTDATED COLLECTION ITEM?

How long does a collection item stay on your credit report? A collection item usually stays on your credit report for seven years. Now, what if a collection item is on your credit report for a debt that was over seven years old? Under the FCRA, you can write a letter to the credit bureau requesting the collection to be removed based on the statute of limitation.

Late Payments

How long does a 30,60,90 late payment stay on your credit report? A late payment usually stays on your credit report for seven years.

We all live in a fast pace society, and sometimes we forget to pay our bills on time. What if you received a letter indicating that you were 30 days past due on your credit card? What are your options at this point? Well, you can allow the item to stay on your credit report for the next seven years, or you can resolve the matter by asking your credit card company to remove the late payment as a courtesy. You can make your request to the creditor via what is known as a goodwill letter.

SAMPLE GOOD WILL LETTER

Your name

Address

Phone number

Date

Company name

Address

To whom it may concern

I have been a customer of your company since (date), and I had always paid my bill on time up until (date) when I unintentionally failed to make my payment on time. As a result, my credit score was adversely affected by this late payment.

I am requesting a goodwill adjustment for this late payment on my account. I have since set up automatic payments on my account to prevent this from occurring again.

Thank You

How to remove a charge off items from your credit report?
What is a charge of item?

You recently obtained a copy of your credit report, and you noticed there was a negative item listed on there as a charge off. Well, what exactly is a charge off item and how long does it stay on your credit report? A charged off item is a debt after an 180 days not paid to the creditor; is deemed uncollectible by the creditor. The lender usually sells this debt to a debt collector; then the debt collector attempt to collect the debt from you. A charge off item can severely negatively impact your credit. So what can you do about it?

Solution

A charge off item usually will remain on your credit report for seven years. So with that in mind what can you do to remove this charge off item from your credit report? Some people rush to pay off the item in a naïve attempt to fix their credit. But once you pay this item it will show up on your credit as a "debt settlement", this may have a negative impact on your credit score. But by taking this action, the seven years will start all again before the item get removed from your credit report.

The best action you can take is to contact the original creditor and ask them to remove the item from your credit report. You should call the original creditor ask them to remove the item in exchange for a monetary payment. If they agree to the offer, you should ask them to send the agreement to you in writing before you make a payment.

How to Remove a Judgment from your credit report?

You recently obtain a copy of your credit report, and you found out that judgment is listed on your credit report. What exactly is a judgment? A judgment is an order signed by a judge that states you owe a debt, and you are legally obligated to pay the debt. It is important to note that a judgment usually stay on your credit report for ten years.

For a judgment to be placed on your credit report, you should have received a summons informing you of a court date. If you did not show up to court then in legal terms you would have a default judgment against you.

What are your options at this point?

Option # 1

If the debt in question does not belong to you, then you can dispute the judgment with the credit bureau.

Option # 2

If you were not served the summons to attend court to defend yourself against the lawsuit, then you can ask the court to reopen your case. A judge would decide the merits of your plea then decide whether or not to reinstate the case. If your request is granted, then you will get an opportunity to come to the court and present your case to the judge.

If the debt belongs to you and it was previously paid then you should bring proof of your payment.

If the debt belongs to you, then you may want to negotiate with the plaintiff's attorney to pay a part or the full amount of the debt in exchange for removing the debt from your credit report. Then you can send a copy of the agreement to the credit bureau and ask them to remove the judgment.

Option # 3

If the debt collection agency that placed the debt on your credit report is out of business, then the debt cannot be verified. You should then send a letter to the credit bureau asking them to prove the judgment listed on your credit report belongs to you.

Can you remove a bankruptcy from your credit report?

Typically bankruptcy stays on your credit report for 7 to 10 years. If the statute of limitations has passed since you filed for bankruptcy and the bankruptcy is still listed on your credit report then you can dispute it.

If you filed for bankruptcy because you were in a bad financial situation, but your financial position, turned from bad to good, then you may want to ask the court to vacate the bankruptcy. If your request is granted, then you can send a copy to the vacated judgment credit bureau and ask them to remove the bankruptcy from your credit report.

If the bankruptcy is within the statute of limitation, then you cannot simply just have it removed.

Can you dispute car repossession?

Car repossessions usually stay on a credit report for seven years, but with that said what can you do about it? Can you dispute a car repossession? It depends if the car repossession that is listed on your credit is legitimate you cannot dispute it. However, in certain states repossession have to done according to the laws of that particular state. If the repossession was not done according to the laws of that state, then you can dispute the repossession with the credit bureaus. You may want to contact an attorney in your state to get more information on this particular subject matter.

Can you dispute a Foreclosure?

If a foreclosure is legitimate, then it will stay on your credit report for seven years. If seven years has passed since the foreclosure has been placed on your credit report, then you can dispute the foreclosure on your credit report.

Your second option is to obtain a copy of your credit report and diligently examine it for inaccurate information about your foreclosure. If you find any incorrect information listed in your credit report, such as the date and amount of your foreclosure, then you can send a letter to your original creditor asking them to correct the information or remove it.

Your next option is to write the credit bureau and ask them to correct any error listed on your report regarding your foreclosure or remove the foreclosure altogether from your credit report.

NEW FICO SCORE MODEL AND YOUR MEDICAL BILLS

Great News! As of August 2014 The Fair Isaac Corporation decided to use a new scoring model called FICO 9, the new scoring model will give less consideration to medical bills in collection, than other types of debt in collection. As a result, consumers with medical collection bills on their credit report should expect to see their FICO score increase as much as 25 points. You can still dispute the collection items and also ask the credit bureaus to verify medical collections that are inaccurate.

Paid Collection Items

As of August 2014 the new FICO 9 scoring model will not consider collection items that were paid off when calculating consumer credit scores. This is additional great news for millions of consumers that have paid collection items on their credit report.

Student Loan Default

Student loan default can have an enormous adverse impact on your credit score and many people affected by this situation often feel hopeless. What actions can you take to address this problem?

1. You can contact your lender and ask about a loan rehabilitation program, the loan rehabilitation program offer to remove the student loan default status from your credit report after you have made nine consecutive on-time payments.

2. You can get your student loan discharged if you are permanently disabled.

3. You can do a loan consolidation plan with your current lender, a loan consolidation plan usually requires for three on time payments to get your loan out of default status. However, this option does not remove the negative information from your credit report.

Tax liens

How to remove a federal tax lien? A federal tax lien is the government claim against your property if you fail to pay your tax debt. This kind of debt can severely damage your credit report and hinder you from obtaining new credit. How do you remove a federal tax lien? If you pay your debt in full, then the IRS usually withdraw the tax lien. You can ask the credit bureau to remove the tax lien after the IRS withdraws the lien.

How to remove a state tax lien? You can pay the bill in full and ask the state to remove the lien. You can also ask the credit bureau to remove the lien once it has been placed in a withdrawn status.

Caution

Here is a word of advice regarding the credit dispute process. The credit bureaus have the right to consider frequent disputes to be frivolous and they might not investigate your dispute. The credit bureaus often deem a dispute to be frivolous if you are disputing the same item more than once.

Also, your dispute can be considered to be frivolous if you provide the same reason for your dispute without sending any supporting documents.

Therefore, you should dispute one or two items each time you make a claim. Also, you should send the credit bureau documents to help support your disputes such as a receipt showing you paid the item in question or a cashed check.

Also, your initial dispute letter should be mild and non-threating. If you have to send more dispute letters to the credit bureaus, then you can use more increasingly bold language to express your rights under the Fair Credit Report Act.

You should keep an organized file with a copy of all correspondence between you, and the credit bureaus. Make sure to send your information via registered mail so you can have proof that you were in contact with them.

Here is a sample initial dispute letter you can send to the credit bureau to remove an inaccurate item from your credit report.

Sample Dispute Letter Step 1

Your name

Address

Date of Birth

Social Security number

I am writing to dispute the following item in my credit file: (Name of company) ABC Collection Company has reported that I have an outstanding collection item for the amount of---------. This debt does not belong to me, and I am respectfully asking for this item to be removed from my credit report.

Thank You

Your Name

What if the credit bureau did not remove the collection item from your credit report?

After you send your dispute letter to the credit bureau, 30 days later you received a response from them stating that the item in question was verified as belong to you.

What should be your next step?

You should contact the collection agency directly requesting them to validate the debt they have listed on your credit report. Here is a sample debt validation letter you can send to the collection agency. Make sure that you send your letter by registered mail so you can have proof you sent the letter to the collection agency and you should also keep a copy of the letter you sent to the collection agency.

Step 2

Your Name
Your Address

Date
Collection Agency
Address

Dear Madam/ Sir

I noticed that your agency is reporting that I owe you a debt. However, I am not aware of this debt. I have the right to validate this debt based on the Fair Debt Collection Practice Act. I would like you to validate this debt by sending me proof that I owe this debt.

Sincerely
Your Name

Step 3

What if the collection agency did not respond to your debt validation letter?

If the collection agency did not reply to your debt validation request, then you can once again contact the credit bureau to explain to them what steps you have taken to validate the debt. Make sure when you write the credit bureau to include a copy of the letter you sent to the collection agency, along with proof your letter was sent by registered mail. Here is a follow dispute sample letter you can send to the credit bureau asking them to remove the collection item.

> Date
> Your Name
> Your Address
>
> Credit Bureau
> Bureau Address
>
> To Whom It May Concern:
>
> I have previously disputed this collection item as inaccurate, but you sent me a letter stating you were able to verify this debt. Therefore, I exercised my rights given to me by the Fair Debt Collection Practice Act and sent a letter via registered mail to the collection agency requesting them to validate the debt. However, the debt was NOT verified by the collection agency.
>
> I also enclosed a copy of the letter I sent to the collection agency along with proof I sent them my letter via registered mail.
>
> The Fair Credit Reporting Act requires you to maintain accurate information in my credit report and for you to verify the disputed item within 30 days. I am once again respectfully requesting for this inaccurate item to be removed from my credit report, or I will exercise my right to sue you in court.

Thank You

Yours Truly

Name

Signature

Here are the addresses for the credit bureaus dispute department.

Equifax

P.O. Box 7404256

Atlanta, GA 30374-0256

Experian

P.O. Box 9701

Allen, TX 75013

Transunion

P.O. Box 2000

Chester, PA 19022-2000

REBUILDING YOUR CREDIT MADE SIMPLE

There are many things in life that will cause someone to have bad credit. However, we will focus on some solutions on how to rebuild your credit.

The most important thing is to keep your credit accounts in good standing. Therefore, you should take great care to pay your credit cards and store cards on time. By paying your credit accounts on time, you will be able to maintain a positive credit history. Some people will naturally ask the obvious question, how can I obtain credit if I have bad credit? The answer is simple; credit is something given based on trust, and a poor credit rating may not earn the confidence of most lenders. However, there are some lenders that are willing to extend credit to people with a bad credit rating. If you have a poor credit score, you can begin to establish a positive credit history by taking one simple step. You can ask a close friend or family member to allow you to become an authorized user on one of their credit cards, that is in good standing.

Most people with a poor credit rating fell into a bad economic situation in the past; some people had late payments, charge off accounts and collection accounts within the last several years.

The best solution to begin cleaning your credit of negative items is to uncover what is in your credit report. Therefore, you should get a copy of your credit report ASAP, and then start searching for items that are outdated. Obsolete items are negative things listed on your credit report that is past the statute of limitations. In most states, the statute of limitation for derogatory listed items on your credit report is seven years. If you have identified negative items on your credit report that are beyond the statute of limitation you can send a letter to the credit bureau and ask to remove the item.

1. Search your credit report for any inaccurate information such as a wrong charge off amounts, incorrect charge off dates and any other incorrect negative item that may damage your credit rating. Your next step is simply to ask the credit bureau reporting the negative item to remove the inaccurate information, according to the Fair Credit Reporting Act.

2. Once the negative things start falling off your credit report, you can expect to start receiving offers in the mail for a new credit

card. You should read the offer very carefully before applying because some of these offers come at a high price in terms of interest rates and annual fees. Also, try to find out what is the minimum credit score someone need to get approved for that particular card. You can find out this information by typing the name of the card in an internet search engine and also typing what is the minimum score to get approved for it.

3. Check your most recent credit report directly online with Equifax, Transunion and Experian to verify if you meet the minimum criteria for that credit offer. Also, make sure you indicate your correct annual income information when applying for a credit card because under-reporting your annual income can cause you to get a decline for the credit card.

4. Keep your current credit card balances under 30% utilization of the debt to credit limit ratio.

5. Avoid paying your bills past the due date because recent late payments can seriously hurt your efforts to rebuild your credit.

6. Develop good spending habits, as a general rule, try only to purchase items on credit you can afford to pay off within 30 days.

7. Consider setting up automatic payments to ensure your bills are paid on time.

8. Do your homework before purchasing anything that requires you to sign a contract such as a car loan. Because when someone with a poor credit rating obtains a car loan their interest tend to be extremely high. A high-interest rate credit card or loan will mostly take away a good portion of your income and can cause you to fall behind on your other obligations. Not to mention if you can't keep up with your car payments then your car can get repossessed. Repossession can severely hinder your efforts when it comes to rebuilding your credit.

a. Your credit history will improve as you begin making on-time payments on your credit accounts, you will then start to receive better credit offers in the mail. Be selective when applying for credit because if you apply for credit too often this will send the wrong message to potential lenders and, as a result, lower your credit rating.

CHAPTER 4

HOW TO STOP COLLECTION AGENCIES DEAD IN THEIR TRACKS!

Are you being harassed by debt collectors? The Fair Debt Collection Practices Act gives you the right from stopping collection agencies from calling or writing you. What exactly is the Fair Debt Collection Practice Act? The FDCPA is a law that was established to eliminate unfair debt collection practices, specifically prohibiting debt collectors from being abusive or deceptive when they are trying to collect a debt. If you are being harassed by a collection agency, you can write a letter merely informing them to stop contacting you. For example, you can state in the letter that based on the Fair Debt Collection Practices Act I am asking your company to cease any attempt to collect this debt. If the debt collector still insists on harassing you, then you can report them to the Federal Trade Commission.

Know your rights

Under the Fair Debt Collection Practices Act
A debt collector may not

Usc obscene language or use threats of violence against you

Falsely claim that they are attorneys or government representatives.

Falsely claim that you have committed a crime

Lie about the amount of money you owe

Falsely claim that they are working for a credit reporting agency

Say you will be arrested if you do not pay your debt

use a fraudulent company name

attempt to collect interest or fees unless they are legally allowed to debt collectors may not lie when they are trying to collect a debt

If your rights have been violated by a debt collector, you sue them in a state or federal court for up to a $1000 for each violation. Your time limit to sue the debt collector is within one year of the date when the violation occurred.

INCOME EXEMPT FROM GARNISHMENT

Social Security Benefits

SSI Benefits

Veterans Benefit

Civil Service and Federal Retirement

Disability Benefits

Military Annuities

Survivors' Benefits

Student Assistance

Railroad Retirement Benefits

Merchant Seamen Wages

Disability Benefits

Foreign Service Retirement

Federal Emergency Management Agency Federal Disaster Assistance

There are exceptions to these wage exemptions. For example, if you owe federal taxes, student loans, child support and alimony then your income can be still garnished.

HOW TO STOP A WAGE GARNISHMENT?

A creditor or a debt collector can get a judgment against you; they can ask a judge to issue an order to garnish your bank account. However, what can you do about it?

If you were not properly served documents indicating you were being sued for a debt by a creditor, then you can ask the court to vacate the judgment and thus stop the garnishment. But you will still have to prove your case in front of the court.

If you already paid the debtor or made a partial payment towards the debt, then you should bring proof to the court.

If the creditor failed to inform you promptly about the garnishment, then you may be able to stop the garnishment.

If a creditor won a judgment against you then in most states they will be required to send you a demand letter. A demand letter is a last chance letter giving you an opportunity to pay or negotiate the debt before your wage or bank account is garnished. Usually when the debt collector uses a Marshall to garnish your salary, then you might have to pay additional fees and interest, plus the original judgment.

You can also ask the debt collector to accept a certain amount of money in exchange for stopping the garnishment.

When a creditor has obtained a judgment against you, many states require them to send you one last warning letter before the garnishment begins. This document is known as a "demand letter." If you get a demand letter from your creditor, don't ignore it. Many lenders rather get payments from debtors rather than deal with the cost and time-consuming paperwork involved with garnishments. Use this opportunity to negotiate a payment plan with the creditor before they begin the garnishment process.

CHAPTER 5

DRAMATICALLY INCREASE YOUR CREDIT SCORE BY OVER 100 POINTS IN AS LITTLE AS 45 DAYS - OR LESS!

1. *How do professional credit repair specialists increase their clients' credit ratings?*

- Keep your credit card usage under 30% of your overall limit.

- Ask your credit card company to increase your credit limit without performing a "hard inquiry". Increasing your credit limit while maintaining or decreasing your credit card balance will often improve your credit score.

- If you have a number of credit cards with small balances such as $20 or $30, pay them off right away. Credit bureaus usually take into consideration how many of your credit cards carry a balance; having too many small balances can count against your credit score.

- Ask a relative or friend with an excellent payment history to add you as an authorized user on their credit card, especially if they have a zero balance or 0% financing.

- Limit the number of loans and credit applications you apply for in a single 6-month period. The only exceptions to this rule are home, auto, or student loans. Credit bureaus usually don't mind if you've applied for many of these types of loans, even within a two-week period.

- Use your old credit cards once in a while to keep them open; creditors sometimes close inactive accounts. If your old credit cards are closed, you lose an important part of your credit history, which can decrease your credit score. Credit bureaus like to see that you've had open lines of credit over many years.

- Dispute any negative or erroneous items on your credit report.

- Maintain a healthy mixture of credit accounts such as credit cards, store cards, and installment loans.

- Apply for new accounts only as needed.

- Transfer your credit card balances to a card with a lower interest rate. Taking this action can increase your credit rating and your overall credit limit.

- Ask credit bureaus to update any credit accounts which you've paid off - but still show an outstanding balance.

- Ask credit bureaus to report any "accounts in good standing" that are not shown on your credit report.

- Ask your creditors to forgive you for any late payments.

- Dispute any "charge off" accounts, late payments, and

collection items on your credit report that don't belong to you.

- Dispute any negative items on your credit report that are more than seven years old.

- Ask your credit card company to increase your credit limit by performing a "self-inquiry". In order words, they can view your credit report as if you had provided them with a copy.

- If you are an authorized user on a card with numerous late payments and a high balance compared to the overall credit limit (over 30% is high), call your creditor and ask them to remove your name from this account.

- Scan your credit report for any unauthorized "hard inquiries", and dispute these with the credit bureaus.

GET A FREE CREDIT REPORT EVERY 7 DAYS!

Wouldn't you like to get 24-hour free credit monitoring, notifications about the best credit offers, and a free copy of your Equifax and Transunion credit reports every seven days?

Believe it or not, you can easily accomplish this feat via a smartphone or tablet app. The "Credit Karma" app tracks your credit score and explains how you can benefit from it. This service provides free credit reports with no hidden costs or obligations. Based on your score, you will gain access to attractive offers from companies that value your creditworthiness.

Your credit score can change daily! Credit Karma currently provides their members with an updated Equifax and Transunion score every seven days. Millions of people consider this free service a vital component of their financial lives.

Knowledge is power! Having the best, up-to-date knowledge of your creditworthiness may help you avoid financial ruin, alert you to any incorrect or fraudulent activities on your accounts, and save you thousands of dollars.

LEARN HOW TO MONITOR YOUR BANK ACCOUNTS, CREDIT CARD ACCOUNTS, BROKERAGE ACCOUNTS, BUDGET YOUR MONEY, AND GET YOUR FREE CREDIT SCORE ALL IN ONE PLACE.

Do you have trouble keeping track of your finances and avoiding costly fees?

In today's fast-paced world, it's easy to forget to pay your bills and get a "late notice" or two. Likewise, you can inadvertently have unauthorized transactions deducted from your accounts. It's easy to miscalculate how money you spend, budget and save – but this can cost you dearly in bank fees!

If you don't pay attention to your accounts, expensive penalties can rob you of your hard-won savings. It takes discipline to save up money to purchase a home, save for your children's future, prepare for retirement, or plan a vacation. Though your savings or CD balance compounds slowly over time, a negative compounding effect can quickly drain your savings – if you get caught in a "downward spiral" of bank penalties and fees.

Mint.com allows users to sync their financial accounts onto one platform via an app (or a convenient website).   Mint allows you to track your spending habits, create monthly budgets, and set savings goals. This service alerts you when your bills almost due; you can even pay bills directly from their website. Mint helps you get your FREE credit score, compare credit card offers, and much more!

CHAPTER 6

OVER 50 INGENIOUS TIPS AND SECRETS TO EFFECTIVELY PROTECT YOURSELF AGAINST POPULAR SCAMS, FRAUD AND IDENTITY THEFT

Do you know how costly identity theft can be?

According to the Federal Trade Commission, identity theft affects approximately 9 million Americans every year. In fact, identity theft is the fastest-growing crime in America. Identity theft has become a **major global problem**; a smart approach and vital information is needed to neutralize this threat.

Consumers' personal information is usually obtained by fraudsters so they can gain access to bank accounts and create fraudulent credit accounts.

If you are the victim of identity theft, you lose your savings, your credit, and your reputation. If you don't handle an identity theft properly and promptly, you can have a very time obtaining credit in the future.

Your chance of becoming a victim of identity theft increases each year. It's only a matter of time before you or someone you know becomes a victim of identity theft. Across the globe, a consumer's identity is stolen every 30 seconds. Thieves open accounts in their victims' names and spend their victims' hard-earned savings on lavish shopping sprees.

Victims, on the other hand, face the painstaking task of recovering their identities. The process of resolving an identity theft with your financial institutions and law enforcement officials takes an average of 33 hours to complete. In addition, victims typically lose over $700 in out-of-pocket expenses while trying to recover their identities.

The bottom line is simple: don't let this happen to you.

TYPES OF IDENTITY THEFT

Do you even know enough about identity theft to start protecting yourself? How do these crimes take place?

Before we explore how to stop identity theft, let's take a look at the various types of identity theft that are currently wreaking havoc on our society:

MEDICAL IDENTITY THEFT: This can occur when someone uses your medical insurance to obtain health care. This type of fraud can have huge consequences for you and your family – both financially and medically. Just imagine if you couldn't receive routine medical care because of conflicting information in your medical insurance records. What if you were suddenly responsible for thousands of dollars' worth of medical bills you had never racked up?

FINANCIAL IDENTITY THEFT: This happens when someone uses your personal information to obtain credit, gain access to your bank account, and compromise you financially in many other ways. The devastating impacts of this type of crime can set you back financially for the rest of your life.

CRIMINAL IDENTITY THEFT: This usually occurs when someone commits a crime and pretends to be you. Just imagine two cops showing up at your job and placing you under arrest for murder. How would you feel knowing that someone committed a crime in your name?

SOCIAL SECURITY IDENTITY THEFT: Along from your name, your social security number is one of the cornerstones of your identity. Your social security number is often used as a "master key" to control access to your financial life. Your social security number can be used to file false tax returns, obtain government benefits in your name, apply for loans and credit cards, obtain a passport, and much more.

IDENTITY CLONING: This occurs when someone literally "becomes you" in everyday life. A criminal can get a job by pretending to be you, attend school in your name, and do a great deal of damage to your reputation.

CHILD IDENTITY THEFT: Identity thieves can use your children's social security numbers to get loans, drivers' licenses, credit cards, steal from the government, and conduct criminal activities.

UTILITY THEFT: Identity thieves may steal your information to obtain electricity, cellular phone, cable, and gas services.

INSURANCE THEFT: Insurance can be obtained in many forms: car insurance, medical insurance, home insurance, health insurance, renters insurance, commercial insurance, and many others. Identity thieves often use your personal information to obtain the insurance they need – at great cost to you!

BUSINESS IDENTITY THEFT: Identity thieves may use your business EIN number to obtain credit, products, and services in your company's name.

OTHER IDENTITY THEFT: One of the most common but overlooked identity thefts is the stealing of information for the purpose of reselling this information on the black market to other identity thieves.

TIPS AND SECRETS FOR EFFECTIVELY PROTECT YOURSELF AGAINST FRAUD AND IDENTITY THEFT

How can you protect your information from a data breach? What steps can you take to prevent fraud and identity theft from turning your life upside down?

Check your credit accounts and bank statements for unusual activity every month.

Enroll your bank and credit accounts for "paperless statements" to avoid theft by mail.

Ask your bank to send you email alerts when the see unusual activity on your credit and bank accounts. This technology allows you to respond immediately to an identity theft – even if you aren't on your computer.

When you order checks, pick them up directly from your bank.

Only carry essential documents with you. Avoid carrying around more credit cards than you need. Leave your social security number, passport, and birth certificate in a safe place.

Sign up for a credit monitoring service that alerts you to suspicious activity on your credit report.

Shred your old bank statements, credit card statements and any other documents that show your personal information.

Don't give out your personal information over the phone unless <u>you placed the call</u> to the company in question.

Choose good passwords for all of your credit and banking accounts. Create a hard-to-guess passwords that use both letters, numbers, and special characters.

If you sell or give away an old computer, phone, or tablet, make sure you delete any and all personal information. Follow the manufacturer's instructions for "wiping" the device's memory.

Don't reply to emails you have not solicited.

If you don't need to apply for credit any time soon, contact the three credit bureaus (Equifax, Transunion, and Experian) to freeze your credit report. This prevents people from opening unauthorized credit accounts in your name.

Keep your personal documents in a safe.

Install a "wire fall" and antivirus protection on your computer to secure your personal information.

Ask the credit bureau to place a security alert on your credit report. This alert requires potential creditors to verify specific information before granting credit in your name.

Inform your bank and credit card company that you would like to use a password to verify your identity whenever you request account information over the phone.

If you are the victim of fraud, ask the credit bureau to add a "seven-year victim" statement to your credit report. This will require potential creditors to call you before issuing credit in your name.

Beware of phishing! Phishing is an attempt to obtain your sensitive information personal data falsely via electronic communication. Phishing scams are usually attempted to get your bank account number, social security number, credit card number, debit card number, username, and passwords. Beware of scam text messages which can appear to be alerts from your financial institution that ask you to click on a link.

Scam texts may ask you to click on a link to reactivate your debit card; this is a dirty trick designed to steal your information.

Change your passwords every couple of months.

Do not use the same password for all of your accounts.

Never leave your personal information in your car.

Create passwords for all of your computers, cell phones, and all electronic devices.

Use extra caution when making purchases online.

Do not use public Wi-Fi to do anything related to financial transactions or that may reveal your personal information.

Look out for "shoulder surfers" when you're at an ATM. Also, be on the alert when using your computer, smartphone, or other electronic devices in public.

Consider purchasing protective screens for your electronic devices that prevent people from seeing your screens while you're using your devices.

You may want purchase an identity theft detection product that help you take a proactive step to safeguard your sensitive information.

Memorize your passwords and other vital personal information; do NOT write them down!

You should NOT put your address and phone number on your checks.

Consider putting your picture on your credit cards.

Never lend anyone your credit or debit cards.

Never discard leave behind your ATM receipts after conducting a transaction.

Properly dispose of your old debit cards, credit cards, and canceled checks.

Use a good shredder to cut your documents into tiny pieces that are not easily reassembled.

Never pin numbers that follow a simple numerical pattern like "1234" or "4321".

Don't use your date of birth, the last four numbers of your social security number, or the last four digits of your phone number as a PIN code.

Don't leave your credit card statements and bank statements in plain sight at your home or place of business.

Don't share an ATM or debit card with a family member. If your card is compromised, it may be difficult to track; and the bank will most likely deny your fraud claim.

Periodically change your online banking and email passwords.

If you have a joint account with your spouse, your online banking user ID and password should be different from theirs.

Use a telephone password for your mobile phone company, bank, and credit card company.

If you strongly suspect your identity may have been compromised, notify your local police department, social security office, bank, medical plan, DMV, IRS center, and post office. Taking these measures can make it difficult for someone to file a tax return, use your health insurance, steal money, obtain credit, or commit a crime in your name.

Obtain free 24-hour credit monitoring from creditkarma.com or creditsesame.com.

Track your phone in case it gets lost or stolen. Get an app that protects the sensitive information on your phone.

Update your outdated phone software. When phone software becomes obsolete, it is quite simple for someone to hack into your device.

Use encryption when sending out an email that contains your sensitive information.

Consider signing up for an identity protection service that offers services like "wallet protection". Wallet protection is an identity theft protection service that minimizes your exposure to fraud when your wallet is lost or stolen. Typically, these services cancel your credit cards if your wallet is lost or stolen.

Review your medical statements to ensure no one is using your health insurance to obtain medical benefits.

Get an ID protection service that offers Black Market Internet Scanning. These services patrol the internet to discover if identity thieves are buying and selling your personal information.

File your tax return early to avoid someone else filing a tax return in your name.

Write to the credit bureaus and opt out of preapproved credit card offers. This limits your chances of someone stealing your mail and applying for credit in your name.

Be careful what information you reveal when you use social media. For example, be careful not to reveal your place of employment, date of birth, or your phone number. This information can be used to track down where you live and could compromise your safety.

Change your Wi-Fi password to something more complex; Cybercriminals seek out victims with easy-to-hack default passwords.

Learn and use the privacy and security settings on your social networks because some social media apps can identify your approximate location in real time.

Be wary of unfamiliar online communication that uses urgent language to convince you to share your information. Cyber criminals often urge their victims to act before thinking.

Be wary of email and online communication that use threatening language to coerce you into complying with a request.

Periodically update your firewall and antivirus software; the outdated software may offer you less cyber security.

WHEN TO USE A CREDIT CARD VS A DEBIT CARD

Do you know which card is best to use?

When you use a debit card, you're giving someone access to the funds in your checking account, which can compromise you financially. Use a credit card when you're on vacation, shopping online, purchasing big-ticket items or eating at a restaurant. When you're dining out at a restaurant, remember that your debit card often leaves your sight. Credit cards typically offer more fraud protection (such as insurance protection for your purchases) than debit cards. Also, debit cards can give fraudsters full access to the cash in your savings account, the available credit on your credit card, and lines of credit. Credit cards and lines of credit are often used as a source of overdraft protection. Just imagine if your debit card was compromised?

QUiCKILY DISCOVER IF YOUR IDENTITY HAS BEEN STOLEN

If you notice any of these "red flags", call your bank and creditors right away:

You receive unexpected calls from debt collectors.

You stop receiving bills in the mail - without notice from your creditors.

You notice unauthorized debits from your checking and credit card accounts.

A place you do business with was recently compromised due to a data breach.

You notice unauthorized "hard inquiries" on your credit report.

Your credit card was inexplicably declined during a routine transaction.

You receive an email from a friend or family member instructing you to send them money.

You receive a phone call from someone telling you they are calling from "the precinct" and you should send them money to bail out a family member or loved one.

Your address and other identifying information on your credit report are changed without your permission.

You receive a credit card you didn't apply for.

You are declined for credit despite having excellent and low debt.

You receive a bill in the mail for something you didn't purchase.

You suddenly stop receiving your mail.

You receive an alert from your credit monitoring agency about a recent unauthorized "hard credit inquiry".

A WORD OF CAUTION

It takes vigilance and proactive thinking to reduce your chances of becoming a victim of fraud and identity theft. Take caution in your everyday life - even during normal activities such as using an ATM. Identity thieves use card reader devices at ATMs to take your personal information and duplicate your debit card.

Don't be afraid to file a police report if you're the victim of an identity crime. Also, don't download phone apps or open and reply to emails from unfamiliar sources. Occasionally erase the "cookies" on your computer, as well as any software that allows your passwords to populate automatically. Be careful who you go to for computer repair; your personal data could be stolen and used to create another identity. Discard your old tablets, laptops, cell phones, and other electronic devices that may contain your personal information with the utmost care

People spend a lot of time on social media; be careful not to reveal too much personal information about yourself and your family. Criminals often "data mine" social media sites to carry out their dubious plots. The average person may unwittingly reveal quite a lot about themselves to strangers.

Social media is often used by those who pretend to be something they're not to win your trust. An internet acquaintance could ask you to send them money, which can lead to thefts. Be careful about the information you provide on online survey forms and websites. You might think you're answering a quick survey to win a computer or an iPhone; however, you might be providing personal information to a scammer.

Single women and men should be careful about the information they reveal on dating sites. How would you feel if a psychopath showed up at your doorstep at three o clock in the morning with a big knife eagerly waiting to do you harm? Scammers also like to offer nonexistent items for sale on popular websites. They do this to obtain your payment information and use it to make unauthorized purchases in your name.

Did you know a person can use your cell number phone to conduct a background check?

Yes, it is true. Your phone number can reveal where you live, who your relatives are, and who your friends are. Consider getting a Google Voice number which don't reveal much of your personal information. You can give this number to new acquaintances and use your primary number with trusted friends and family members.

CHAPTER 7

39 MOST COMMON ASKED QUESTIONS ABOUT CREDIT

What is a credit inquiry?

Answer: When you apply for credit you must give the potential lender permission to obtain your credit report.

When a lender obtains a copy of your credit report from the credit bureau, this information will get recorded on your credit report as an inquiry. The inquiry will show who received a copy of your credit report and when they received this information.

Can I obtain credit without doing an inquiry?

Answer: You typically have to do a credit inquiry to obtain credit from a lender. However, they may extend credit to you at their discretion without doing a credit inquiry.

How many points does an inquiry take off your credit score?

Answer: An average a credit inquiry will take off anywhere from 2 to 3 points from your credit score?

How long does an inquiry stay on my credit report?

Answer: A credit inquiry will stay on your credit for two years.

How long does a collection item remain on your credit report?

Answer: A collection item usually will remain on someone credit report for seven years.

How long will a bankruptcy remain on my credit report?

Answer: It depends on the type of bankruptcy that was filed, for example, Chapter 13 bankruptcy will stay on your credit for seven years while Chapter 7 bankruptcy will remain on your credit for ten years.

Can I qualify for a mortgage with bad credit?

Answer: it's possible to be eligible for a mortgage with bad credit, however, be prepared to pay a much higher interest rate.

How long does a late payment stay on your credit report?

Answer: A late payment usually will remain for seven years on a person credit report.

How long a student loan default will remain on your credit report?

Answer: A federal student loan default can remain indefinitely on your credit report until it is taken out of default status. There are loan repayment programs that offer the borrower an opportunity to take the loan out of default by making nine consecutive payments. The portion of the unpaid balance is then sold to another lender, and then the default student loan status will be removed from your credit report.

What score do I need to become a first-time home buyer?

Answer: The majority of lenders will require a minimum credit score of 620 to approve a first-time home buyer for a mortgage.

What credit score do I need to refinance my current mortgage?

Answer: Certain types of residential mortgages do not require a minimum credit score. You should check with your current mortgage lender to find out if you qualify for a Harp Loan. Otherwise, a credit score of 680 and above might help you to be eligible for a mortgage refinance.

What credit score do I need for an auto loan?

Answer: A 550 credit score may help you qualify for an auto loan, but you will most likely pay between 9% and 14% on your car loan.

How is my auto insurance score determined?

Answer: Your driving record along with your financial history will be used to calculate your auto insurance score.

What information is in my credit report?

Answer: You should expect to find identifying information such as your name, current and previous address, employment information, and date of birth, telephone number, a part of your social security number, your credit history, public records and credit inquiries.

If I check my credit report will this hurt my score?

Answer: No. You can check your credit report as often as you like without lowering your score. Your credit score will decrease when you attempt to obtain credit and the potential lender run your credit.

Does my spouse information appear on my credit report?

Answer: Your credit report will contain only your information unless you have a joint account or an authorized user account with your spouse.

How can I get a free copy of my credit report?

Answer: By federal law you are entitled to a free copy of your credit report annually. You can obtain a copy of your credit report at www.annualcreditreport.com or call 1 877 322 8228.

If I close an old credit account will this affect my credit score?

Answer: Most likely it will affect your credit score, because your credit score calculation take into consideration the length of your credit history and when you close an old account you will also lose the history that is associated with that account.

Can my employer get my credit report?

Answer: only If you give them your approval.

Can any random person or company get a copy of my credit report?

Answer: No. Only someone or a company with a legitimate business reason can obtain a copy of your credit report.

Do I have a right to know why I was denied for credit?

Answer: Yes. If you are denied credit, then you should receive a notification on why you were denied credit. Your right to receive this information is based on the Equal Credit Opportunity Act.

When should the credit bureau respond to a credit report dispute?

Answer: The credit bureau has 30 days to investigate your dispute but if you send the credit bureau more information during the 30 day dispute then the credit bureau will have an additional 15 days to investigate your dispute.

Where should I send my credit report dispute letter?

Equifax
P.O. 7404256
Atlanta, GA 30374-0256

Experian
P.O. Box 9701
Allen, TX 75013

Transunion
P.O. Box 2000
Chester, PA 19022-2000

What is a charge-off account?

Answer: After an 180 of not paying a credit account the creditor then writes off that debt as a loss. However, they will still attempt to collect that debt.

Can I remove a collection item from my credit report by paying it off?

Answer: No. Unless the original creditor agree to remove the item, otherwise the item will be listed as paid in full, and the item will remain on your credit report for an additional 7 years from the date it was paid.

How long does car repossession stay on my credit report?

Answer: 7 years

How long will a foreclosure remain on my credit report?

Answer: 7 years

What are the easiest inaccurate items to dispute on my credit report?
Easiest

Late payments

Outdated negative items over seven years

Charge-offs

Collections

Inquiry

What is a good credit score?
Answer: A good credit score is considered between 690 and 720.

How to build your credit after bankruptcy?
Answer: Get a secure credit card from a bank that offer this product, make sure you pay all your bills on time, apply for a retail card or a gas card and get added as an authorized user to a credit account with an excellent payment history.

Can I remove myself removed as an authorized user from a credit card account?
Answer: Yes you or the account holder can ask the creditor to remove you from the account as an authorized user.

If I pay off my credit cards will it hurt my credit?
Answer: No. In fact, it looks good on your credit report to be able to pay off your revolving debt in full.

How many credit cards do I need?

Answer: It is wise to take on the right amount of credit cards you can handle, therefore on average five credit cards should be enough for most people.

What is not in my FICO credit score?

Answer: race, age, color, sex, marital status, occupation, national origin and employment history.

What is re-aging?

Answer: If you make a payment on a debt that is about to reach the statute of limitation then the statute of limitation will start all again. For example, if you had a credit card in a collection that item would typically come off your credit report in 7 years. But if you made a payment towards the collection item after three years then you will have to wait an additional seven years before this item is removed from your credit report.

If I check my credit report will my credit score go down?

Answer: No, you can do a self-inquiry as many times as you like without lowering your credit score.

Can I build my credit history by making my rent payments on time?

Answer: Yes, rental payments can help you establish and build a credit history.

Can a negative credit score affect the possibility of me getting a job?

Answer: Yes, some employers view a negative credit report as a warning sign and an indication how a candidate might perform in their role.

Can a bad credit score prevent me from establishing a bank account?

Answer: Yes, A bad credit score can cause a bank to deny your request to establish a new account. Some banks perform a credit check and a Chex system inquiry when a potential customer comes into the bank to open an account.

What is Chex Systems?

Answer: Chex Systems is a consumer reporting agency that keeps information on people who abuse their checking accounts and engage in fraudulent activities.

CHAPTER 8

MOST COMMON ERRORS FOUND IN CREDIT REPORTS AND HOW TO AVOID THEM

According to the federal trade commission, 1 in 5 Americans has a mistake on their credit report. In other words approximately 40 million Americans have an error on their credit report; this number is not only astounding, but it is very revealing. Therefore, a lot of people are being denied credit based on inaccurate information found on their credit file. Also, some people are paying high-interest rates based on errors found that were found in their credit reports.

Three common mistakes that cause errors on credit reports

- Sometimes people inadvertently provide the wrong social security number when applying for credit.

- People at times make a mistake when they enter your information on a credit application.

- An account that belong to John Smith Sr sometimes will get reported as owned by John Smith Jr

Top common errors found in credit reports

Incorrect names

Wrong address

Wrong social security number

Accounts NOT belonging to you

Accounts with the incorrect credit limit

Open accounts being reported as closed

Closed accounts being reported as open

Account incorrectly reported as being late

Outdated information

The mixture of the two different credit reports

Identity theft

An account listed twice

Incorrect phone number

Authorized user listed as the owner of an account

Ex-spouse information listed on credit report

Incorrect account status

How to prevent common errors on your credit report?

It can be very disheartening to discover that you might have errors on your credit report, but taking steps to prevent errors from being placed on your credit report can help you to avoid a lot of unnecessary stress. The first step a person should take to prevent errors on their credit report is to obtain a copy of your credit report at least once a year and review it very carefully. Take extra caution to secure yourself against identity theft. You should consider setting up credit monitoring alerts to inform you whenever a recent update has been made to your credit report, act fast to correct any errors on your credit report and double check any information you provide to a creditor when you apply for credit.

CHAPTER 9

LITTLE KNOWN FACTS ABOUT CREDIT

BENEFITS OF OWNING A HOME

The benefits of owning your home are impressive. For example, when you are a homeowner you build equity with each payment you make towards your mortgage. Also your home value usually increases over time, you and your family get more privacy, your property tax, and interest on your mortgage payment is a tax deduction, you can build a solid credit history by making your mortgage payments on time, you don't have to worry about rent increases and if you need to you might be able to take out a home equity loan.

STEPS TO HOME OWNERSHIP

Step1. Check your credit report for any errors, negative items, and inaccurate information. Your next step is to dispute any negative items and inaccurate information on your credit report. You should pay down your credit card balances down to 30% or less so you can improve your debt to limit ratio. When you reduce your debt to limit ratio on your credit cards, your credit score will most likely increase. When your credit score increases, you will most likely qualify for a lower interest rate on your mortgage.

CHECK YOUR INCOME, WORK HISTORY AND HOW MUCH YOU QUALIFY FOR.

Step2. On average a bank like to see at least two years of steady employment from a client applying for a mortgage. Also, use an online mortgage calculator to find out the loan amount you might be able to afford. If you are a first-time home buyer, you may be eligible for a

Federal Housing Administration (FHA) mortgage. An FHA mortgage requires 3.5 percent down payment versus a 20 percent down payment on a conventional mortgage. It is also important to know that the Federal Housing Administration will understand certain past credit problems such as collection items, late payments, and even a previous bankruptcy. You can still even qualify for an FHA loan with a 620 credit score and still receive a low rate on your mortgage. However, if you had any federal tax liens or student loan default, then you will not be eligible for an FHA loan.

Step3. Speak with you bank loan officer to find out about the requirements to qualify for a mortgage and to help you decide the type of mortgage that best suit your needs.

Step 4.
Find a Real Estate Agent

Do your homework when you are looking for a Real Estate Agent. You should take care to find someone who will be patient enough to help you find your dream home and to guide you properly throughout the home buying process.

Step 5.
Begin looking for your home

Make sure you carefully select a home that meets your criteria. Also, a thorough inspection should be conducted on the house prior to closing because the last thing you would want is to get stuck with a house in poor condition.

CREDIT CARDS SECRETS REVEALED

The first step when applying for a credit card is knowing the actual purpose why you are choosing to apply for a credit card in the first place. Some people find credit cards with cash reward to be very attractive. While other people may want to apply for a credit card offering a 12 to 18-month intro of 0% interest rate, so they can make purchases without paying interest for a specific time and take advantage of balance transfers. There are many more reasons why consumers apply for credit cards, but it is important to know the ins and outs about credit card so you can make well-informed decisions.

One of the most important things a consumer should know before applying for a credit card is their credit score. Understanding what your credit score is can put you in the driver's seat when you are determining which is the best credit card for you. Consumers with excellent credit usually qualify for the best offers, but having average to poor credit often means a consumer will pay higher interest rates and possibly hefty annual fees.

UNDERSTANDING INTEREST RATES

So you recently applied for a credit card offering 0% for 6months, fast forward two weeks later you checked your mail and there it is your brand new credit card with a $5000 limit. You are thrilled because you were planning on using the credit card to book a trip to Cancun and pay off the card over the next five months. So you wasted no time to book your ticket and hotel room; you also purchased things you think are necessary for your trips such as new clothes and shoes. Before long your credit card balance jumped up to $4,500, but not to worry about now because you are planning on paying off your debt before the six-month intro zero percent grace period expires. Unfortunately, you were not able to pay off your credit card before the six-month interest grace period. To make matters worse, you were only making a minimum payment of approximately $105 every month. But six months later your minimum payments were being applied to the interest and principal on your credit card balance, instead of being applied to just the principal balance. Therefore, if you were to keep making the minimum payment of $105 it would have taken you 56 months to pay off the credit card. You would have also paid approximately $1,280 in interest payments.

ANNUAL PERCENTAGE RATE

When you initially applied for a credit card your annual percentage rate (APR) was 11.24%. However, what does this all mean to you? The APR is the annual cost of borrowing money from your credit card. The APR specifically applies to the interest rate that will be charged, if your credit card balance is not paid in full on or before the due date.

TYPES OF APR

There are usually several types of APR that applies to your credit card account. For example, there is an APR for purchases. There is an APR for cash advance, balance transfers; there is an APR that usually goes into effect when you make a late payment or if you violate any other terms of your credit card agreement.

CAN MY CREDIT CARD RATE INCREASE

Your credit card rate can increase if a promotional rate has expired, your credit card rate can increase when you don't follow your credit card terms, when changes are made to a debt management plan and if your variable rate increases. What exactly is a debt management plan?

A debt management plan is an official agreement between a creditor and a debtor pertaining to a debt owed to the creditor by the debtor. The program is also designed to help the borrower pay off his or her outstanding debt faster. A debt management plan or debt relief plan is often a service a third party company offers to someone who cannot afford to pay their debts on unsecured accounts. The third party company (debt relief company) will collect the payment from the debtor and then distribute it to the creditor. A debtor often uses a debt relief company, because the company may help them to evaluate their debt, help the debtor to come up with a budget, establish a time frame to pay off their debt and negotiate with creditors on their behalf.

A debtor usually enters into a debt management plan with a creditor

ADVANCED CREDIT REPAIR SECRETS REVEALED

when they are facing some financial hardship that makes it difficult for them to make even the minimum payments on their loan or credit card. The debt management plan will most likely include an agreement to allow the debtor to make an affordable payment to the creditor. The creditor will probably agree to dramatically reduce the interest rate on the debtor balance or outright eliminate the interest on the debtor balance.

What kind debts are excluded from a debt management plan?

A debt management plan usually does not include debts such as auto loans, student loans, mortgages and home equity.

Disadvantages of a debt management plan

A debt management plan is not legally binding; therefore your creditors can still sue you while you are enrolled in the program. Your wage can still be garnished if the creditor gets a judgment against you. Also, when a debtor enters into a debt management plan his or her credit cards must be closed, and the debtor cannot obtain a credit card.

How will debt management affect my credit?

Debt management will most likely hurt your credit score. Because when you enter into a debt management program, you will close your credit card accounts and possibly lose some or all of your account's history.

Can a debt management save my credit?

Yes, debt management can help lower your payments by allowing you to make an affordable payment towards your outstanding balance. Therefore, the plan may help you avoid defaulting on your debts. Defaulting on your debts may end up putting your debt into collection and collection can have a devastating effect on your credit score.

Defaulting on your debts can have a far worse effect on your credit than entering into a debt management plan.

What is credit card insurance and how can it help me?

What if you were not able to pay your credit bills due to loss of employment? Wouldn't be nice if your credit card company could make your monthly payments for you? Credit card insurance plans are voluntary programs that offer to pay the bill of a cardholder in particular circumstances.

The main types of credit card insurances are:

- Unemployment insurance offers to make the minimum payment on a card credit holder's bill for a specified time frame, this type of coverage usually cover you if you are laid off from work, but it does not apply if you voluntary quit your job or get fired.

- Disability insurance is a coverage offered by credit card companies in the event you have a medical disability; the company will make the minimum payment on your bill.

- Life insurance for credit card holder offers to pay off the balance of the credit card if the cardholder passes away.

- Property insurance covers the merchandise that was bought with your credit card; the coverage will only apply if the property was stolen or accidentally damaged. Please note there are some restrictions that apply to this type of credit card insurance. You should ask your credit card company for an explanation of their property insurance coverage so you can make an informed decision whether to purchase this type of insurance.

How much does it cost?

On average credit card insurance will cost approximately 2 % of your balance. For example, if you had a credit card balance of $2000 your insurance payment would be $200.

Do I really need it?

Only you can answer that question but most importantly, life is unpredictable for the most part. Therefore, credit card insurance may serve its purpose. But you may want to use credit cards when only necessary and pay off your balance in full every month to avoid interest fees.

Does it protect my credit?

Credit card insurance has its benefits and in certain circumstances it may help to make on time payments to your credit card company. Making on-time payments towards your credit card will help you to maintain a positive credit history.

How to increase your credit card limit without getting a credit inquiry?

You have had a credit card with a $500 limit for the past three years, but you would like to increase your card limit, but you are concerned that a credit inquiry will decrease your credit score. How can you potentially increase your credit card limit without getting an inquiry on your credit report? Some credit card companies will allow you to perform a self-inquiry on your credit report through their telephone automation system.

A self-inquiry will let your credit card company gain access to your credit report without lowering your credit score. Because you can run your credit (perform a self-inquiry) as many times as you like without lowering your credit score. Once your credit card company evaluates your credit, they will make a decision immediately or within 30 days to approve or deny your request for a credit card limit increase.

HOW TO LOWER YOUR CREDIT CARD INTEREST RATE?

The easiest way to reduce your credit card interest rate is to apply for a card offering a zero percent interest rate on balance transfers. The second option is to learn about some of the promotions other credit card companies are offering. Then, call your current credit card company and ask to speak with a supervisor, once you have a supervisor on the phone inform him or her how long you have been a customer with an account in good standing. Also, mention some of the current credit cards with attractive interest rates their competitors are currently offering, and then ask politely for a lower interest rate on your credit card. This strategy may or may not work however it is worth a try.

MARRIAGE AND CREDIT

Marriage is one of the most important parts of someone life; however there are certain things you should be aware when it comes to credit and marriage.

You can ask your spouse to add you as an authorize user on his or her credit card to help build your credit.

Being married does not mean you will automatically get your spouse good or bad credit history.

If you are purchasing a home together, then both spouse credit history will be taken into consideration. If one spouse have great credit and the other spouse has bad credit, then the spouse with the bad credit will weigh heavily on the interest rate.

Also, if you take your spouse last name, your credit history will not vanish. Your credit report will update to reflect your new name.

Joint account holder VS authorized user when it comes to marriage. Both spouses are equally responsible for making on-time payments on joint credit accounts. On authorized user accounts, only the primary account holder is responsible for making on-time payments.

HOW TO KEEP DIVORCE FROM DESTROYING YOUR CREDIT

Divorce can be the one of the most traumatic and stressful time of someone life, but that doesn't mean your credit should get ruin as well. Here are some help tips to stop divorce from severely damaging your credit:

Remove your name from any credit account where you are listed as an authorized user. Taking this action would help protect your credit if your ex-spouse decided to max out the card and not pay the bill.

Close joint accounts. Closing your joint accounts can help you if your ex-spouse is delinquent on those accounts.

Sell properties that belong to you and your ex-spouse. Taking this step is important because if your property goes into foreclosure your credit rating will take a deep dive.

Remove your name from joint bank accounts, because if your ex-spouse has a judgment against his or her name then your account can be frozen.

If you have a joint installment loan or an auto loan, then you should consider refinancing the loan into just one of your names.

Check your credit to ensure your ex-spouse debts are not on your credit report.

HOW TO OBTAIN BUSINESS CREDIT?

The foundation for getting business credit is having an excellent personal credit history. When business owners apply for a company credit card or a business loan, their credit score will weigh heavily on them getting approved.

If you are applying for a loan as a corporation then having a deposit account in good standing with your financial institution might also help you to obtain credit from them.

The other component for obtaining business credit is operating a company with a good track record of paying its bills on time, avoid having the business's bills going into collection and avoiding judgments placed on your business.

Also, some banks may consider the length of time your company has been in business. The bank may examine the risk associated with the industry your business operates in, the profitability of your business and the type of assets your company has will be taken into consideration as well. These things might vary depending on the amount of your loan request.

You can also obtain a copy of your business credit report from experian. com, equifax.com, and dnb.com.

RESOURCE

SAMPLE DEBT VALIDATION LETTER

Your Name

Your Address

Date

Collection Agency

 Address

Dear Madam/ Sir

I noticed that your agency is reporting that I owe you a debt. However, I am not aware of this debt. I have the right to validate this debt based on the Fair Debt Collection Practice Act. I would like you to prove this debt belong to me, by sending me proof that I owe this debt.

Sincerely

Your Name

SAMPLE DISPUTE LETTER

Your name

Address

Date of Birth

Social Security number

I am writing to dispute the following item in my credit file: ABC Collections Company has reported that I have an outstanding collection item for the amount of---------. This debt does not belong to me, and I am respectfully asking for this item to be removed from my credit report.

Thank You

Your Name

SAMPLE GOOD WILL LETTER

Your name

Address

Phone number

Date

Company name

Address

To whom it may concern

I have been a customer of your company since (date), and I had always paid my bill on time up until (date) when I unintentionally failed to make my payment on time. As a result, my credit score was adversely affected by this late payment.

I am requesting a goodwill adjustment for this late payment on my account. I have since set up automatic payments on my account to prevent this from occurring again.

Thank You

SAMPLE DEBT SETTLEMENT LETTER

Your name

Address

Phone number

Debt collection company name

Address

To whom it may concern

Account number

I would like an opportunity to resolve this outstanding debt owed to your company as soon as possible. I am offering x amount of dollars to settle my debt entirely.

Also, I would like you to remove all late payments comments associated with this debt from my credit report.

I may not be able to make another offer such as this one, because of my current financial obligations.

If you agree to the terms of this letter, then please sign it and return a copy of it to me. Once I receive a signed copy of this letter then I will pay you x amount of dollars in the form of a bank check or money order.

SAMPLE CEASE AND DESISTS LETTER TO COLLECTION AGENCY

Debt Collector

Address

City, State & Zip

Date:

Re: (Account Number)

To Whom It May Concern:

I am exercising my right under the Fair Debt Collection Practices Act by asking your company to cease all communication with me. Furthermore please do not contact my job, and my family members as well. If you violate my rights under the Fair Debt Collection Practices Act, then I will sue you for $1000 each time you communicate with me.

Yours Truly

SUMMARY OF YOUR RIGHTS UNDER THE EQUAL CREDIT OPPORTUNITY ACT

You should not be denied credit because of your race, sex, marital status, age, religion if you receive public assistance. You should not be asked for information regarding your spouse, except: if your spouse is applying with you on a joint credit application. If your husband or wife will be allowed to use the account, if you depend on your spouse's income or alimony or child support income from a former husband or wife, if you live in a community property state. You should not be asked if you receive alimony, child support, or separate maintenance payments unless you first volunteer that information. You do not have to provide this information if you do not depend on child support, alimony, or separate payments to get credit. A creditor can ask if you have to pay alimony, child support, or separate maintenance payments.

When Deciding To Approve You for Credit Or When establishing The Terms Of Credit, Creditors May Not

- Consider the racial makeup of the neighborhood where you want to buy, refinance or improve a house with the money you are borrowing.

When Evaluating Your Income, Creditors May Not:

- Disregard income because of your sex or marital status. For example, a creditor may not count a man's salary at 100 percent and a woman's at 80 percent. A creditor may not come to a conclusion that a woman of childbearing age will stop working to raise children.

- Decline to include income because it comes from part-time employment, Social Security, pensions, or annuities.

- Decline to consider reliable alimony, child support, or separate maintenance payments. A creditor may ask you for evidence that you get this income on a regular basis.

You have the right to:

- receive credit without a cosigner if you meet the lender's requirements.

- have a cosigner other than your husband or wife.

- Know whether your application was accepted or rejected within 30 days of filing a complete application.

- Know why your application was rejected.

- Learn the particular reason you were offered fewer favorable terms than what you requested

- Find out why your account was closed or why the terms of the account were made less favorable. Taking this step might be possible if your account was inactive, or if you failed to make payments as agreed.

TRUTH IN LENDING

The Truth in Lending (TILA) protects consumers against inaccurate and unfair credit billing and credit card practices. It requires lenders to provide consumers with loan cost information so that consumers can make comparisons and shop for certain types of loans.

SUMMARY OF YOUR RIGHTS UNDER THE FAIR CREDIT REPORTING ACT:

The federal Fair Credit Reporting Act encourages the accuracy, fairness, and privacy of information in the files of the credit bureaus. You must be told if the information in your file has been used against you. You should be told if someone uses a credit report or another type of consumer report to deny your application for credit, insurance, or employment or to take another adverse action against you. The creditor must tell you, and must give you the name, address, and phone number of the agency that provided the information.

You have the right to know what is in your credit report if:

If a person or company has taken adverse action against you because of information in your credit report; if you are the victim of identity theft, if your credit file contains inaccurate information as a result of fraud; if you are on public assistance; if you are unemployed but expect to apply for employment within 60 days

You have the right to ask for a credit score.

You have the right to contest any incomplete or inaccurate information.

Credit bureaus must correct or delete any inaccurate, incomplete, or unverifiable information within 30 days.

Consumer reporting agencies may not report obsolete negative information. A consumer reporting agency may not report negative information that is more than seven years old, or bankruptcies that are more than ten years old.

Access to your file is limited. A consumer reporting agency may provide information about you only to people with a valid need -- usually to consider an application with a creditor, insurer, employer, landlord, or other business. The FCRA specifies those with a valid need for access. You must give your consent for reports to be given to employers.

For more information, visit www.ftc.gov/credit.

SUMMARY OF THE FAIR DEBT COLLECTION PRACTICE ACT

A debt collector cannot make any false, deceptive or misleading statements.

A debt collector cannot falsely represent a character, the amount or legal status of the debt.

A debt collector cannot falsely represent himself/herself as an attorney.

A debt collector cannot state or imply that non-payment will result in arrest or criminal prosecution.

A debt collector cannot threaten suit, garnishment or seizure of property without the legal ability to do so.

A Debt collector cannot report or threaten to report false credit information.

The act provides a general prohibition against the use of any unfair or unconscionable means to collect a debt.

A debt collector cannot attempt to collect any amount not authorized by the agreement creating the debt or permitted by law.

A debt collector cannot accept or solicit post dated check without providing written notice of at least three days that intends to deposit.

A debt collector cannot accept or solicit postdated check for the purpose of threatening criminal prosecution.

A debt collector shall provide the following notices:

Initial communication (oral or written): "This communication is from a debt collector in an attempt to collect a debt. Any information obtained will be used for that purpose.

Each subsequent communication: "This communication is from a debt collector," or "this is an attempt to collect a debt."

Within five days of the initial communication (oral or written), in writing:

- Amount of the debt
- Name of the creditor owed
- Right to dispute the validity of the debt within 30 days
- Name and address of the original creditor
- If disputed by a consumer within 30 days, the collector will provide verification of the debt.

You have the right to sue a debt collector if they are in violation of your rights. You can sue in state or federal court.

A debtor's who does not want to request validation, does not waive any right the debtor might have to deny validity at a letter date and to tell a debtor that failing to respond will verify the validity of the debt violates FDCPA.

A debt collection letter can be deem as deceptive under the FDCPA even if it only implies that it is a law firm.